learning
to
love
myself

alex aubrey

ISBN: 9798388058805

chapters

learning to love myself

stuck

and

unhappy

it is the hardest thing
to learn
how to be alone
again

i don't know how
i found myself here
but it is what i do from here
that will make all the difference

my biggest fear
is never being loved
the way i want to be loved

why am i
going through all these
healing
only to get myself
broken again

the same person
can't hurt me twice
but i've been hurt
the same way
by too many people

people come and go
but hurting
seems to be a feeling
i can't shake

no matter what i do
i still end up
back at the same spot

questioning myself
questioning my worth
was it me
or was it them?

how many times
can i do this
if nothing
is going to change

i am so tired
of starting over
trying something different
but still leaving with
the same disappointment

ask yourself
why are you still holding on?
does it feel good
or is it just familiar?

you've come too far
to settle
for anything less than
what you want

you know
you need to leave
when the thought of it
makes you feel relieved

if you really like someone
being friends with them
is better than dating them

- advice from my dad

you know exactly
what you need to do
to improve
but you are not doing it

- *self-sabotage*

if you keep waiting
for change
you will always
be waiting

which is more unforgiving
you hurting me
or me staying on
despite it?

nothing
has hurt me more
than my own
expectations

i don't think
i can do this anymore
but what if
i am wrong?

it is never too late
to start treating yourself
the way you deserve

i know
you have been hurting
and i'm sorry
it will continue to hurt
yes
it will keep hurting for awhile

i can't promise
that you will find
the version of yourself
before you were ruined
but i know
change will come
and you are going to
get through this

it will keep hurting
until one day
it will finally stop

your old self
burnt
your new self
relentless
and you will be okay again
and you will be okay again

promise me this
never let anyone
shame you
for choosing yourself

when you are
no longer surprised
just exhausted,
that is when
you need to let go

nothing is worth staying
if you are not happy

i think about leaving
and there was a huge
sigh of relief

- *i think that says a lot*

you will never
meet anyone else
who will be as good for you
as yourself

you know
you can do better
you are just waiting
for a sign

but how many more signs
do you need
for you to know
what you already knew?

if it hurts you
it is not right

i am afraid
of losing you
but i am even more afraid
of losing myself

- *i can't do this anymore*

it is not
your responsibility
to fix the ones
who leave you broken

you live your best life
when you do exactly
what you want
and you stop apologizing for it

at the end of it all
remember this
if you ever find yourself
in a place
where you are truly unhappy
remember
you always have the option
to leave

all i know is that
in a few years
everything will be fine

you will be in my life
no longer
and i won't be in yours

i will no longer know your number
but i will still remember *biscuit*
your wide-eyed puppy
i will wonder how she's doing
but i won't ask

i will remember
how i used to love you
and getting over you
will still be the hardest thing
i ever had to do

the thing about people
is they change
sometimes about who they are
and sometimes about what they want

it was unfortunate
when you decided that
you didn't want me

but i know that in a few years
everything will be fine
this will bother me no longer
and wherever i am
i hope i am happy

and genuinely,
i hope by then
i can wish the same
for you

i don't want
half of anything
give me everything
or don't give it to me
at all

you deserve
to be loved by someone
who will love you
unconditionally
exactly
as you are

- *don't ever change yourself for someone else*

i know some nights
it feels like
it will never be
the same again

and the truth is
maybe you are right
it won't be the same
ever again

and you know what
maybe that's not a bad thing
at all

you will get over this moment
and better things will
come into your life

and you will be happier
and you will be happier

sometimes
good things come to an end
because
we aren't ready

it took me a long time
to get here
i don't want to
lose myself again

i think i can forgive you
if i let this go
but i know
i will never forgive myself
if i don't let go

learning to love myself

learning

to

let go

you end up with
what you tolerate

if you don't like something
you can always leave

we accept
what we think we deserve
but there is no limit
on what you can become

stop
trying
to
please
everyone

you can't keep pouring
into a broken cup
you will empty yourself
and the cup will still be
empty

stop shrinking
yourself
to fit
other people

life is short
stop wasting time
on toxic people

not every loss
is bad
sometimes
it sets you free

stop choosing
what isn't choosing you

if it's not mutual
what is the point?

stop trying to make it
what it used to be
the past is in the past
let it be what it is

let the good times
be good times
and let yourself move forward
when it is over

it is okay
to let go of people
who do not make you
feel good

you can't heal
if you don't let yourself feel

the thing
you are so scared of
is going to
change your life

it is okay
to outgrow people
and it is okay
if they outgrow you

- *people come and go*

finding happiness
within yourself
is the only way
to be truly free

stop expecting honesty
from people
who lie to themselves

choose the people
who choose you
and let go of the people
who let go of you

you are scared
because it matters

- *do what is best for you*

the only limitations
are the ones
we put on ourselves

nobody is coming
to save you.

save yourself.

it is time
to let go of people
who have let go of you

there is still time
for you to be
who you want to be

- *don't give up*

there will come a day
where you think more
about the present
than the past

stop saying yes
when you want to
say no

stop talking yourself
out of the things
you wish could happen

if you avoid it
you will never get it

if you are happy
you will know it

being content
isn't doing something
and forcing yourself
to be okay with it

you break a pattern
when you learn to
respond differently

i'm sorry to myself
for holding on so tightly
when i already know
i needed to let go

if they don't respect you,
it's over

i thought you were the one
i needed the most
turns out i was wrong,
it was myself

no one is coming
stop expecting
someone else
to save you

- *you are your own savior*

stop hurting yourself
over people
who don't care
about you

if they wanted to,
they would

you can overthink yourself
to death
and they wouldn't care
they wouldn't even know

move forward
if it's meant to be
it will come back
otherwise,
it doesn't matter
anyway

i will not spend
one more year
doing the same shit

- *promise to myself*

you have to
fall in love
with yourself
first

i know it's pretty fucking difficult. i know it hurts like hell. i know you have a million thoughts in your head and you're repeating the same questions over and over. i know it feels like this pain will be forever and right now there is nothing ahead of you but darkness. i know you feel like you might not make it through. i know a part of you is questioning if it's even worth making it through. i know. tonight will be difficult as hell. and so will tomorrow. and maybe the night after. but hey you know what? you've been through this before. and you can do this again. you know you got this in you. i believe in you. you will get through it. you will get over it. just like all the times before. you will be fine. you will be okay.

sometimes
growth means
leaving people behind

i want you to know
that this is about me
and not about you

and i want you to know
that it will never be about you
ever again

today
i release you
from my mind
i will imprison you
no more

letting you go
was the beginning of me
learning to love myself

learning to love myself

learning

to love

myself

the hard times
you are going through now
will teach you everything
you need to know
later in life

forgive yourself
for the mistakes
you've made when
you didn't know better

you are still healing
from the things
you didn't deserve
and that's okay

- *keep going*

one day at a time.
one step at a time.

you do not need
anything more
than that

don't give up
you will find yourself again
and it will be better
than the version
you were before

take all the time
you need
to simply
just be yourself

7 steps to self care:

1. if it feels wrong, don't do it.
2. say exactly what is on your mind.
3. trust your intuition.
4. never speak bad about yourself.
5. don't be afraid to say yes.
6. don't be afraid to say no.
7. love openly and loudly.

don't chase after love
chase after life instead
and life
will love you back

it is okay
to compromise sometimes
it is better to bend a little
than to break

let your love
be stronger
than your anger

stop beating yourself up
over things
that don't matter anymore

you don't need
to be productive
all the time

some days
it's good enough
to simply exist

stop comparing yourself
with the other versions of you
in parallel universes,
you are here
and that is wonderfully enough

it is never
too late
to figure out
who you are

speak your truth
even if it makes others
uncomfortable

they can hurt you
but they can't ruin you

but is it a loss
or is it a redirection?

remember
you can start again
over and over
as often as you need

your competition
isn't other people

it is being better than your past
focusing on your present
and not over analyzing the future

you can be happy
for other people
without feeling terrible
about yourself

7 ways to feel better:

1. go out for a walk and breathe deeply.
2. find a new recipe and cook a homemade meal.
3. dress up. make yourself look good. even if you're staying at home.
4. bake some cookies.
5. try out a home workout on YouTube.
6. look through your photo albums and find 20 photos to print out.
7. get a new journal and just write. fill the whole thing up.

let yourself feel
all your emotions
without labeling it
in any way

instead of a "to do" list
make a "stop doing" list

stop chasing
and start attracting

whatever belongs to you
will simply find you

you have something
others don't,
you care

and that is why
it hurt sometimes
when you care too much
for the wrong person

but that is also why
you will be happy
one day
when you finally find someone
who will care for you
the way you care for them

keep caring
don't let a few jerks
ruin
your preciousness

be nice to people
everyone has
a struggle
you don't see

energy doesn't lie
believe in what you receive
and what you give out

i don't need anyone
to do my healing for me
give me space
and i will do it myself

the best closure
is knowing that
you've tried your best

you are surviving today
and that will be
good enough

give yourself
the power
to become
who you want to be

you have yet to see
the best version
of yourself

there is still so much
you can do
with this life
if only you could
allow yourself to

be enough
for yourself first
everyone else
can wait

once you let go of
all the things you are holding
that do not belong to you
that's when you can
find your way back
to yourself

learning to love myself

by letting you go
i have saved myself

become the person you would fall in love with. someone who would ask the barista how their day is going. someone who would hold the door open for the person behind them. someone who would give their spare change to the homeless person at the train station. someone who would let other cars merge into their lane when driving. someone who would pay for a stranger's coffee. someone who would compliment others on their outfits. someone who would stick their tongue out at babies. someone with really cool hobbies. someone who would paint at the park. someone who would make music in their bedroom. someone who would volunteer at the pet shelter on weekends. become the person you would fall in love with. become that someone. and that will be the beginning of you loving yourself.

dear me in 6 months,
i will make you
fucking proud

learning to love myself

you are

your own

home

stop carrying
old feelings
into new experiences

leave the past
in the past

what is meant for you
is already happening
be patient,
and trust the process

not everything
that is happening
is good
but everything will work out
in your favor
eventually

you will always
find your way back
to yourself

- *you are your home*

the person
you are becoming
is more important
than the person
you have been

don't you ever
fucking apologize
for being yourself

start
by building a relationship
with yourself

there is so much
you can do
within your own company

take yourself to coffee shops
watch a film on your own
visit a museum
and leave after 10 mins
if that's what you want to

there is no pressure
and endless possibilities

say hi to people on the streets
ask the person sat next to you
how their day is going
or say no
if someone approaches you
and you don't want to talk

you can be whoever you want
you can say whatever you want
or nothing at all
there is only one rule
do whatever you want
as long as it is genuine

you exist
and therefore,
you matter

if you survived today,
it is good enough

- *you don't always need to do more*

taking care of yourself
at your worst
is the bravest thing
you can ever do

fresh flowers. handwritten letters. thrift shops.
small local cafes. love poems. neck kisses.
annotated books. ocean waves. postcards. late
night driving. rooftops.

- little things i love

the savior i've been looking for
has been myself all along

i am slowly learning
how to just be in this moment
how to exist
how to understand that
i cannot control everything
i can only experience
all the good and all the good
some i will laugh at
some i will cry through
some i will be confused
some i will adore
i am slowly learning
to welcome it all
and to accept
myself

it's okay. you can let go of all the weight you've
been carrying now. you are okay. you are okay.

if it comes,
let it come

if it goes,
let it go

- *way of life*

your intuition
is always there for you
trust it.

i hope you know
you are capable of
achieving anything
you wish for

i was fine before you
and i will be fine after

today, i choose to let go. i choose to let go of the people who have let go of me. i choose to let go of people who make me overthink and question myself. i choose to let go of people who do not give me joy. today, i choose to be happy. i choose to stay away from any kinds of toxicity. i choose to release myself from all the aches i've put myself through. i choose to give myself the love i so generously give to others. today, i choose to stop hurting myself. i choose to follow positivity and not drown in my own sadness anymore. i choose to embrace openness and not build up walls around myself. i choose to accept and embrace my flaws and grow from them. today, i choose to heal. i choose to forgive myself for all the mistakes i've made when i didn't know better. i choose to guard my soul. i choose to move forward. today, i choose to be brave. i choose to say no to the things i don't want to say yes to. i choose to walk away from places i have outgrown. i choose to value my own time.

today, i choose to love myself.

change
looks
beautiful
on
you

be proud
of the progress
you are making
no matter how small

- *don't give up*

give yourself
the same patience
you give others

the answer
was right in front of me
all along

- *it was myself*

i saw
what i did not have
and decide that
i do not need it

be proud
of what you have
been through

the person you were
one year ago
is so different than
who you are now

you've overcame
so much adversities
know that
you can do this again
you've got it in you

one year from now
you will grow into
a better version
of yourself

your worth
is not determined
by anyone else's
opinion

i haven't been myself
for weeks
and i'm not sure
if i want it back

- change is good

everything i want
is on its way to me

everything i need
is already within me

it takes all the courage
in the world
to love yourself
after all you've been through

- *i'm so proud of you*

you
are
doing
fucking
great

today i am in love
with my life
and all the possibilities
i can do from here

i am so grateful
that i didn't end up
with what i thought
i wanted

learning to love myself

learning to love myself

Made in United States
Troutdale, OR
07/01/2023

10922817R10086